# BEING WITH ME WILL HELP YOU LEARN

## LEARN

By Thomas McColl

Listen Softly London
333 Muswell Hill Broadway
London
N10 1BY

ListenSoftlyLondon.com
@ListenSoftlyLDN

BEING WITH ME WILL HELP YOU LEARN
COPYRIGHT © 2015 by Thomas McColl

First Edition, October 2015

Cover Design by Aaron Lipschitz
Edited by Dominic Stevenson
Typeset by Aaron Lipschitz

ISBN: 978-0-9935353-0-7

Published in the United Kingdom

# DEDICATION

To the person who gave me the title of this collection (even though, after you said it, you made me learn the hard way)...

...and, as ever, to F.C.

# Contents

# I

For assuming that I am the most important person in the
human race,
the gods have announced demotion of my I to lower case.

i have not been told when this will take place,
but by stating that, i realise now there is no need.
i have begun my sentence in the previous sentence.

The gods and Descartes in Nirvana have decreed
i think (only of myself),
therefore i am (no longer denoted by a capital i).

i cannot hear the difference,
but i can see the gods have made me half the i i used to be.

i, Claudius. Damn! The gods are not fooled by an alias.

How vain must e.e. cummings have been,
to pay so dearly for his crime?

The gods have informed me
i will be allowed
an exclamation mark for good behaviour
while i am serving out my time.

An i followed by an exclamation mark
is almost a capital i, just once removed.

As soon as my application
to be the most important person
in the human race has been approved,
i'll demand back my capital i
complete with exclamation mark as compensation,
so everyone can clearly see
the gods at last are pleased with me.

# Takeaway Poetry Joint

Hello sir.

Thank you for calling the Takeaway Poetry Joint.

Before we go any further, I would just like to inform you that today's special offer is one free bottle of drink and portion of garlic bread with any large poem, plus free delivery by a performance poet.

I know, sounds good, doesn't it?

Do you have our menu there in front of you?

Yes, it's a long list, isn't it?

The 'Full English' we like to call it – everything from Alvarez to Zephaniah...which, when you think about it, takes you both from A to Z and from A to B – if you get my drift.

Yes sir, you're in a rush, I understand.

Yes, I can certainly make a suggestion. Perhaps you'd like to choose Ted Hughes, deep pan? With this one there's a choice of four different toppings: There's "Pike", part of our 'sag belly' promotion (two for the price of one), or "Thistles" (though we only suggest you try this if you have a rubber tongue), or "Crow", a cheesy myth (albeit well-done), or, finally, "The Jaguar", with which we're offering a pass for two to see the real thing (be completely unaware it's in a cage) at the local zoo.

No, none of these suit you?

Oh, you'd prefer something lighter.

How about Michael Rosen, thin and crispy? With that we have the "Don't Put Mustard in the Custard" topping.

Yes, this one has both mustard and custard, sir.

I know: They say don't, but we do. That's what we're like at the Takeaway Poetry Joint...

You'd like that one?

Great! No probs.

A brave, but excellent, choice Sir. And the poet who's doing the delivery is Thomas McColl.

Yes, *Thomas McColl.*

If he's longer than fifteen minutes you get your money back. But trust me, sir, with this particular dish, he should be no more than a minute or two.

# Open Mic

I went to an open mic poetry night,
read my poems to rapturous applause,
promoted my booklet,
did not sell a single one.

The following week,
I was back on the open mic,
filled my five minute slot
simply by repeating:
*"16 AA batteries for a pound,*
*16 for a pound"*,
and by the end had sold
one hundred packs.

# The Gamble Account

When I opened a new gamble account,
to supplement my current account,
the bank sent me a different kind of card
to the usual plastic one.
It was the Four of Clubs.

I found the nearest cashpoint,
inserted the card
keyed in my personal number.
The Queen of Hearts
and Three of Spades
came up upon the screen.
Seventeen.

I took the print out and went straight to the cashier's desk.
I placed my bet – sixty pounds.
Surely I'd win this time.
The cashier dealt the cards:
The Jack of Diamonds,
Two of Clubs
and Six of Hearts.
Damn! Eighteen.

*"Better luck next time, sir,"* the cashier said, smiling,
as I paid in sixty pounds
to the non-withdrawable gamble account.

# Resignation

I primed the office clock
like a hand grenade
by pulling off the hands

then, ripping out the batteries,
which fell to the ground like spent cartridges,
replaced them with the signed note
stating: *"I resign"*,
clicked the cover shut,
and threw the clock.

It smashed into pieces
when it hit the closed door of the manager's office.

Livid, he came storming out,
only to stop and gawp at the smashed clock,
his face surveying the scene
and registering shock
at losing the round shield
he'd always used to make
his advance towards my desk
with another deadline-heavy
tick, piece of work, tock.

He then looked up and saw me coming towards him,
holding the clock's hour hand in my fist like a knife.

# Self-Discovery

Dave, on his lunch-break,
falls asleep at the rest room table
then wakes up to find his head buried
in page three of his copy of The Sun.

Seeing, from the clock, that he's overslept,
Dave rushes back to his desk,
and it isn't until an hour has passed,
when he goes to the loo,
that he notices the newsprint all over his face,
the headline *Phwoar!* across his forehead,
and a large pair of breasts framing his eyes
so that, for the first time,
a pair of nipples that he's gawping at
are gawping back at him.

He tries desperately to wash it all off,
but can't. Horrified,
what shocks him most
is that no-one there in the office
had noticed anything different.

# Chip Shop Aquariums

Last night,
at the local chip shop,

the server,
thrusting his bare arms
into the vats of boiling oil,

screamed at the cold, cruel world
that made him go insane,

and like a million piranha fish
in schools of bubbling frenzy,
the vicious viscous liquid
ate his flesh.

In chip shop aquariums,
the fish are dead
but the liquid in each tank is alive.

This all makes sense
in a world gone mad.

# The Silent Call

The silent call is never silent.

It rings persistently to get her out of bed,
continuing to ring
until she answers it.

The caller makes no sound.

A budgerigar and rattling cage
she always hears
at the other end before the click.

Dead.

She replaces the handset,
then tries to go back to sleep but can't,

can't get out of her mind
the budgerigar inside the rattling cage,
with useless, flapping wings,
trapped and terrified,
unable to escape the caller's gaze.

# S

There was a young man,
totally obsessed,
who loved the letter S.

He was an S terrorist –
sent chain letters through the post.
One hundred Ss,
complete with message which said:
*"Add one more S and send it on – or else."*

He wrote a book called S
(The word count
exactly one hundred thousand Ss),
sent it out,
and nine months later
was accepted by the young head
of a publishing house
who had a fetish for the letter S.

They eventually married –
It was all S and no love.
But that, for them both, was enough.

# A Warning to all EC Pedestrians

A forthcoming EC regulation states
that all pedestrians must wear number plates
attached to their belts
or on a chain around their waist.

Also, prominent L-plates must be worn
by those who haven't yet passed
the Green Cross Code.

Pedestrians planning to cross the road
must have, as standard,
an air bag beneath their clothes
which will blow up on impact.

Please note that every pavement,
even those along a busy street,
will have a speed limit of three miles an hour.
Any pedestrian caught breaking it
will be banned from wearing shoes for a week
and have to walk in their bare feet.

Any pedestrian caught standing still
for more than fifteen minutes
will automatically receive a parking ticket
(Those stood at bus stops are exempt).

# The Nose Picker: Public Enemy Number One

Last night, police sealed off the end of my street, where a young man was stood alone at the bus stop. He was told to take his finger slowly away from his nose, and as soon as he did, he was surrounded and restrained while forensic experts, quickly on the scene, still putting on their rubber gloves as they jumped from the back of their van, wiped his finger clean of mucus.

They took the sample back to the lab and filed it under the young man's name. From now on, they'll be able to check it against any discarded mucus found in a public place.

This morning, his poster is on the shelter at the bus stop, a blow up of the mug shot taken at the station.

The photo shows him with his finger up his nose. Below it is the warning to a hygiene conscious public:

*"This man is dangerous: Approach with caution. Do not shake his hand."*

# EXTRACT FROM POLICE REPORT:
## Operation 'Stolen Time'

"…We searched the premises
and found two cases filled with boxes,
each containing a one minute unit of Class-A GMT.

The owner of the flat
told us that the units were encased
in seals of solid gravity,
but failed to mention the booby-trap.

It was triggered by DC Burton.
The seals exploded,
and the escaping minutes filled the room,
turning what was simply a split second for the world outside
into a gruelling five hour moment
here in the flat.

The loss of such vital evidence was a major set-back.
Our longer than anticipated dawn raid
had been made
after Scotland Yard received reports
that pretty girls in short skirts
were situated at strategic points
along the length of Oxford Street
pretending to represent a major consumer group,
and asking each passing man they'd greet
for a minute of his time.

The girls were in fact working for the King of crime,
an evil megalomaniac,
known in the underworld as Carl the Clock,
on account of his early days spent fencing Rolex watches,
and each segment of time,
stolen from the unsuspecting men on Oxford Street,
had been converted into a saleable commodity,
though how Carl managed this is not yet known.

Thomas McColl  **19**

The word on the street
is that Carl has fled abroad
and is right now planning the theft
of every spare second
in his host country's time zone."

# In Search of Pedestrianland

Every pavement's made of yellow brick.

Cars are driven by demons
sent by the wicked witch.

The scarecrow feels inferior
for he hasn't yet learned to drive.

The cowardly lion's
still too frightened
to cross the road
to reach the other side.

And the tin man drives a flash new car,
shows he hasn't got a heart,
endangering lives by ignoring the red light,
and never stopping at the zebra crossing.

The witch's cauldron,
full of bubbling tar,
makes new roads
that bring the cars
with grumbling engines
and foul exhausts,
polluting the air we breathe.

The only dreamer left on Earth is Dorothy:

While the scarecrow's off to see the wizard,
who runs a driving school on Baker Street,
Dorothy makes do with the Good Fairy's magic boots,
and lives inside her head
in fantasy Pedestrianland,
where the cars and motorbikes she hates so much
are banned.

# Bucking Broncos

In cowboy country,
seats on all the trains
have been replaced
by bucking broncos.

Experienced cowboys
are able to grip with one hand,
and in the other hold and read
the Herald Tribune,
while pensioners
and pregnant women
have to stand.

A sign upon each bucking bronco reads:
COWBOYS ONLY.
Even during rush hour,
a cowboy does not need to fight for a seat,
he has to fight to stay on a seat.

# Dr X and Miss Y

Last week police raided the practice of Dr X, a renowned expert in the field of acupuncture, and found a pin-struck wax doll made in the exact image of the surgery's wealthiest celebrity client, a Miss Y, who'd been tipped off that the sharp pains she thought were caused by migraines were something worse, and was shelling out money simply to be cured of Dr X's voodoo curse.

Dr X was taken into custody, and charged with obtaining money by deception, and causing CBH: Cursed Bodily Harm.

He wasn't there for long, however. Miss Y, as soon as she took one look at the doll's uncanny but unflattering likeness, requested all charges be dropped, and served an injunction to make sure that photo publication of the voodoo doll was stopped.

She said the doll looked nothing like her, and so could not have caused the pain, and accepted Dr X's explanation that he'd simply found the effigy in a gift shop while on holiday in Haiti.

The following day, the migraines, which had ceased, were back, and driven almost insane, Miss Y rushed back to Dr X, to once more enlist his help in easing the terrible pain.

# The Price of Fame

Struggling actor sold his soul to the Devil, who became his agent and landed him the starring role in a movie playing a blind man who had no arms but could paint great works of art with his feet, and the actor won a BAFTA, but failed to thank the Devil in his acceptance speech, so the Devil came to his home the next day and tore off his arms and gouged out his eyes, and the arms, chopped up into tiny portions, were served as chicken nuggets at a home for the blind in Eastbourne, and the actor's number one fan, seeing the film for the seventh time, was so engrossed in his performance, she failed to notice that she was eating eyeballs with her popcorn.

# Muslim Girl at the Bus Stop

Muslim girl at the bus stop,
wearing hijab and headphones,

full length skirt and colourful top,
respecting Allah and listening to hip-hop,

the fingers of her left hand
click to the beat of the tune,

the fingers of her right hand
adjust the veil, keep it in place,

covering her hair
and perfectly framing her beautiful face.

# Fragments

You've become, as memory fades, blue eyes, piercing, lost in the space of my mind. Your face is elsewhere, your legs and thighs soft footsteps that patter across the wooden floor. And in the bathroom at the end of that hallway – through mist that was then just condensation but now is the passing of time – there's the silhouette of your hand behind the shower curtain turning the tap, the glimpse of a smile through the chink, the sparkling droplets on your naked back, and your name I'm writing with my finger on the mirror but can't now remember.

# Parasailor

Heart attack at 200 metres.

His body,
safely harnessed into a parachute,
descends,

and the round shadow,
like a black spotlight,
passes over unsuspecting friends.

They're cheering as he lands,

knowing that he's safe
in the trained instructor's hands.

# Moon Lee

Moon Lee, you like to play around with death.

You make it look cute.

You dress it up in a short skirt,
a panda sweater,
and a dinky Hello Kitty beanie hat with a bobble on top.

To you, death is light, cheap and fizzy like candy pop.

You are a killing machine.
When death cries out for more,
you place a blood-soaked dummy in its mouth.

You are thirty six,
but look as young as you did at sweet sixteen.
It is said you never age,
for the Devil himself is afraid to meet you.

Moon Lee, you are invincible.
Even on that inevitable day,
when you find yourself at death's door,
you'll be asking if it wants to come out and play.

# Kelly

At Mass, the priest,
bearing down on us
with the Virgin Mary
and the Sacred Heart,
from his pulpit
was too high up to see
Kelly, sat beside me,
stroke my leg,
bring her hand around
the inside of my thigh.

He talked of heaven
while I thought of earth,
for now, my racing heart
was no more sacred,
as my virgin eyes
enjoyed the sight,
inside my mind,
of Kelly, totally naked.

# Robot

I'm programmed to speak a million languages,
when here in this city they speak just one:
the one million and first.

I constantly malfunction:
Sometimes I de-activate,
my head slumps,
will remain like this for minutes at a time,
at work, in the street, alone in my bed-sit.

Oil constantly seeps through my eyes,
and down my face.

I do not always wake
when the alarm clock sounds
and passes through my head
its loud electric current.

My wires are frayed and burnt.

My pain cartridge, flashing red,
will not eject,

and I'm set to self-destruct
for failing to find the woman
who needed my help.

Her desperate plea,
imploring me to bring the code to break the lock,
I've played back so often through my mind's eye,
her image is fuzzy and vague.

Her voice is running
like a virus through my head:

You've left it too late.
You've left it too late.
You've left it too late.

# Nicotine

There are seven sacraments:

The first is baptism,
conducted hidden behind the bike sheds.

The second is confession,
when your mum finds the packet
in your school blazer jacket.

The third is holy communion,
when you learn to breathe in the smoke.

The fourth is confirmation,
when you start smoking fags
with pints of lager down the pub.

The fifth, marriage, is addiction.

The sixth is holy orders,
attained by the newsagent.
He is ordained to marry off the packs of fags
to all the youngsters keen to follow the herd.

And the seventh, last rites,
is there for the chosen third.

# Skulls

A week ago,
I watched, on MTV,
a hem-stressed teenage muzak queen,
with hippie-hick trill
and sleight-of-mouth fake radiant smile,
lip-sync her hit "You've got to love yourself" –
but so ill with image pressure
that she already had this anorexic-bone-set pout
which made her, in close up,
look like a dancing skull with airbrushed skin.

Then yesterday,
on UKTV History,
a Hutu-created cache of crated skulls
shot a spark-shock fear of death
right through my couch-malfunctioned frame.
It was chilling to see
how death could be so easily fused with pop:
Carrying radios,
machete-wielding youths were swept along,
in front of Western TV crews,
by a buoyantly catchy anti-Tutsi song.

It's bizarre,
but I'm seeing, today, on BBC4,
an image of a cracked skull and shattered jaw,
as archeologists excavate a burial site.
Then, suddenly, the programme switches
from the scene of what's believed to have been
a Moon-God pagan worship rite –
complete with a phalanx of drums
preserved in peat –
to a stark reconstruction,
showing a bloody human sacrifice
in time to a murderous beat.

# Sweat Shop

In Isan,
a sub-contracted province,
women – migraine-zeroed,
mouths as dry as the parched plains
on which their mothers worked –
have found that even their spool-tight minds
are unravelled by the foreman's steely gaze.

Through each vowed-silent twelve hour hex,
they work their vein-dead fingers to the bone,
as safety-catchless
Singers drone
and sun-bled windows cast expanding shadows
of the metal grills like nets across the neutered faces.

Five drunken hacks in Phuket sing:
*"The foreman's gait,*
*the endless seam,*
*the sweat-shop is a journalist's dream."*

From Isan, through Phuket, to London,
at a sweat-stitch label's flag-ship store,
a girth-maddened girl –
belt-brained and vacuous –
stiletto-stabs the floor,
as a plumed assistant
breaks the news:
*"I'm sorry, but there's no more*
*of the 10 (that fits your 12) size."*
Over the speakers, a muzak pop group
sings the wrong-belt-buckle blues,
while a stale-eyed boyfriend –
raked of all patience,
bulged with bags,

sighing a stream of lies –
pretends he loves still
his swell-shocked girlfriend's
ever-expanding thighs.

On the bus, she gawps at photographs,
which illustrate a token serious article –
on sweat shops and their workers –
in her glossy fashion magazine.

*"The women, look how slim they are,"* she cries.

# The Queen of Dooley Street

Liz wears a crown of curlers
but the whole world ignores her,
even her plants,
which bow instead towards the sun.

The only fanfare she gets
is the sound of BBC Radio One
turned on at full blast
by her teenage son.

Her husband, the prince,
hurriedly arranged a state visit
to Australia with a younger woman.
That was five years ago,
and she hasn't heard from him since.

Her daughter,
who's made a new life too,
not in Australia but Aberdeen,
no longer tunes in
to see Mum's regal drunken speech on Christmas Day.
She hardly visits at all.

Liz wishes she could have the old days back,
but with her husband gone,
the royal guard's increased
to a chain and two new fitted locks.
The only servants,
a dishwasher and vacuum cleaner,
the only red carpet treatment she gets
is Shake and Vac on two for one.

The front room's gilt framed mirror
no longer paints a kind portrait.
It's been so long since Liz had a boyfriend,

if she walked out with one now,
*'Oh imagine the paparazzi,*
*all along the street,*
*peeking through their nets and curtains,*
*their eyes blinking like camera shutters*
*in disbelief'.*

Liz wishes she could abdicate,
but her house is owned by the State,
she still depends on the civil list of the DSS,
and while replete with the drab majesty of poverty,
she'll remain the Queen of Dooley Street.

# Green Graffiti

Buds, arranged to spell "Fuck U",
have sprouted up along the edge
of every flower-bed in our local park.

Police psychologists conclude
that this spate of horticultural graffiti
has been committed by a lone teenage individual
whose background is an explosive mix
of broken home and well-kept garden.

# The Banshees by the Railway Track

From my bedroom window, I watch the naked banshees comb their golden hair.

They sit in a shallow ditch beside the railway track, their lives an endless dull routine of being forced to comb their hair each time the express train hurtles by.

It doesn't seem to bother them much, and they've certainly endured much worse in recent times:

Each banshee has air-gun pellets embedded in her back, and one was crushed when three boys dropped a concrete block on her from the overhead foot-bridge, simply because they wanted to see if they could crush a banshee's head as easily as they could a melon.

A week later, all three boys were killed in a joy-riding accident as they went too quickly round a bend where banshees had been known to congregate.

An air-gun was found in the boot of the car.

The parents, however, don't believe in banshees and are convinced it was the police in pursuit that caused their children to die.

Who knows – but, in any event, the boys are dead and, once again, the banshees' only problem is the endless dull routine of being forced to comb their hair each time the express train hurtles by.

# Now Showing: EAST LONDON BY NIGHT

There's no plot,
but it starts
at the Manor Park Library bus stop
when I jump on,
swipe my card,
take my seat
beside my personal cinema window screen,
and watch as the film, "East London by Night",
gets under way.
A searing portrayal of urban decay,
each bus shelter advert
a commercial break
from the film's bleak landscape.

# Springtime in Soho

Anyone walking through Soho in winter
cannot miss,
that even in a telephone box,
dark and dank and stinking of piss,
it's somehow always spring.

All year round each day of the week,
lust germinates and flowers into blooms:
flimsy pieces of card,
with blu-tack roots,
so weak they never last
much more than a couple of hours.

The prospects for survival of this species
would be bleak
if it wasn't for all the hovering men.

Just off Brewer Street,
inside a telephone box cocoon,
a man's already mutated
into something that his wife would never recognise:
a strange hybrid creature,
with a human face
but a pair of bulging compound eyes.

A husband,
driven no longer by mutual love and respect
but by the single-mindedness of an insect.

And, all over Soho,
the same thing's happening too
to scores of other men,
ensuring that tomorrow
it will start all over again.

# Classified Secret Service Report on Moral/ Immoral

MORAL and IMMORAL are both vast organisations, operating in each country networks of spies and agents concerned solely with each other's overthrow and destruction. Agents are everywhere – everyone's involved – working undercover in every occupation, in every pub, in every household, on every street, watching, collating, reporting their information.

All that's known for sure about the two groups is that the one side will oppose whatever the other side supports. On both sides, secrecy is essential. Agents often do not even know which side they're working for. Orders are given in the press through coded messages, and people only have to read and take them in to be recruited, often not knowing why it is they've become involved, or where it was they got their orders from.

Double agents are numerous. It's thought most members of IMMORAL still retain MORAL membership, and it's not known how many members each organisation has. Once, it was believed that IMMORAL membership was almost universal within MORAL, but now it's thought that MORAL has managed to infiltrate IMMORAL so effectively, if its own members were taken away there would be nothing left. It's even been rumoured that the two organisations are simply one and the same.

Double agents are sometimes dealt with by a third organisation called AMORAL, that owes its allegiance to neither side, but works for both, and is currently supplying drugs into IMMORAL at their request in order to flush out the double agents and pretenders within its organisation. These noxious, mind-bending drugs, if taken by double agents, twist their minds so much, they render their reports incomprehensible. But even so, though drug use now is compulsory within the ranks of IMMORAL, MORAL has found that its members who've infiltrated aren't being driven out and back into its own camp as expected. Instead, these double agents are dabbling and, getting hooked, are giving IMMORAL more control than ever before, enabling it to infiltrate MORAL from within its own organisation and, at the same time, prevent information leaking out – or at least in any intelligible form.

However, there's concern within IMMORAL that this latest success will make its membership almost redundant in its fight against MORAL, which instead is being won by AMORAL drugs, and making it seem more likely than ever before that the end of MORAL could mean the end of IMMORAL too. AMORAL though concedes that its agents also work for MORAL, using methods MORAL would not use, to combat the spread of drugs, and has agents too who work for neither side, sabotaging the efforts of both. It's also thought that AMORAL is heavily infiltrated by both IMMORAL and MORAL, and would collapse if the two organisations they claim to use and work against suddenly ceased to exist.

# Spiritual Appraisal

This poem does not have a sign above it
saying "Confessional".

And though I know that priests
have been known sometimes
to read modern poetry,
and after years of experience
know a good sin when they hear one,
I won't be confessing mine
in this poem at least.

Instead, I have them listed in another poem
which is kept under lock and key,
and if I ever have a spiritual re-awakening,
I'll mail it to the parish priest
of my local diocese,
complete with stamped addressed envelope
for him to send me back his absolution,
and hopefully too an answer to my written question:

*Dear Father,*
*are these sins bad and interesting enough*
*in your opinion*
*to warrant their publication?*

# Cardboard Crime

Dean Scanlon returned home
to find his furniture not just stolen
but replaced by cardboard replicas,
all held together by sellotape.

Each clock he had
was replaced as well
with a cardboard face,
on which was etched
the time of ten o'clock in felt-tip pen,
the time it's believed the crime took place.

The thief, or thieves, got in
by breaking the back door window pane,
and even had time
to replace the broken glass
with a made-to-measure cardboard square.

This morning,
police raided a suspect's house,
but all they came across
was a life-size cardboard cut-out,
with the face blanked out.

# The Chalk Fairy

Each night I traipse
the streets of London,
drawing chalk lines
round homeless people
sleeping rough.

I've found
that, even in the early hours
of Christmas Day,
there's no shortage of bodies
to draw my outlines round:
London's one big crime scene
every single day of the year.

# Funny Money

For some reason,
the Bank of England Governor
decided it would be a good idea
to start printing jokes
on the back of banknotes.

In a surprise speech to assorted industry chiefs,
he said he wished
to *"stuff the Bank of England's stuffy image,*
*and make people*
*look at money in a different way."*

TV comedian Bobby Casserole
was brought in to lead a think-tank,
but all Bobby did was lead the think-tank
down to the nearest All Bar One,
and soon the expense account was bled dry,
with only one joke thought up,
which Bobby, facing the Board of Directors,
began to crack in a slurry voice:
*"How many Bank of England Governors*
*does it take to change a light-bulb?"*

Bobby was kicked out on to the street
before he could even deliver the punch-line.

The Governor apparently thought
that Bobby was just a two-bit comic,
but after a national outcry,
the Governor was forced to resign.
Within weeks,
Bobby had a ghost-written book out, called:
*'The Bank of England Governor – My Part in his Downfall',*
and made a million pounds worth of banknotes,
which the Bank of England had to pay on demand,
with or without his jokes.

# Smile

Today, the street hawker's selling knocked off smiles from an old battered suitcase in front of Camden station:

*"Hey darling! Why the long face? Come over here and get a smile from my suitcase. What do you mean, the smile I sold you last week has begun to fade? My smiles ain't fake. Didn't you read the packet? 'Happiness not supplied'. You gotta keep recharging your batteries, love. But don't worry, I've got just the thing for you – happy pills, three for the price of two..."*

# Noise Nazi

The head of the SS (Sound System)
Division "Das Noise"
lives next door,
harassing me and the neighbours,
invading our rooms
in every flat on every floor,
to terrorise and ruin lives
regardless of age,
from old ladies to children,
the hard of hearing even.
Armed with a decibel ton assault
on the senses,
howitzers disguised as speakers
rain down a barrage of noise.

Sometimes his Nazi parties
go on from dusk till dawn.
All night long,
residents bury their heads
underneath their pillows,
but know it does no good.
His terror is complete.
He is the plague
of Benwell council estate.

His name is Obergruppenführer Rick.
He thinks he owns the whole estate,
and ask him to turn his music down,
even just a bit,
and he'll tell you just to go to hell,
then turn the music up still more.

This man commands an army's worth of sound.
He makes his noise to terrorise
with pounding jack boot beats.

# The Naturist

No one knows
I posed
for a naturist magazine
as soon as I turned eighteen.

I chose the setting:
The lush green ancient forest of Epping
where, who knows, long ago,
more kingly men than me,
in their emperor's new clothes,
may well have swung free
through the undergrowth.
At 5am, with the silence broken only
by the early morning bird-calls,
there I was, running bare,
kicking leaves,
feeling the breeze around my balls.

My desire for exhibitionism peaked
when I streaked
down our street
and back again at midnight
as part of a drunken bet.

That was last week,
and I was apprehended by an off-duty officer
who, with his girlfriend,
was returning home from a nearby pub.

I'm due to appear in court,
and I don't care that I've been caught,
or how it might be viewed
when I brazenly declare
that, yes, I've even modelled in the nude.

# Wedding Poem (for Joe and Laura)

The two of you walk on sure ground.
Trouble ahead is just a lamppost to walk round,
and remember: there's no need to unlink
just to walk through its shadow.

And if pressure brings
the darkness down,
still marvel at the sight
of the angler fish's light:
There's beauty in even the ugliest things.

For I know each heart
without the other
would be as bereft
as the sad impression left
by a stolen work of art.

Your love for each other is real
expressed not just today in public
but in private too
as invisible ink that forms on the skin
from the heart's tattoo
that only ultra-loving eyes can see,

and both of you always knew
that you'd end up here on this day,
that the soothsayers and charlatans
are not worth wasting money on.

Today, you make your vows because of love
and not astrology.
The stars can align, shine,
or fall to the ground like confetti.
It's not written there,
but within both your hearts,
where true love clearly is.

# Petrus Bonus Lombardus (1290-1351)

Petrus Bonus Lombardus
is an alchemist
who ignores his shadow
as it toils in vain
to get blood from the stone
of the damp stagnant cold walls
in his ever more dilapidated
dank and draughty
castle home.

He ignores his young wife too,
who knows now,
as she looks down
at her painfully thin and chapped hand,
that the wedding ring of pure gold
was nothing but gold plate
that's worn away to reveal
a worthless alloy metal band.

Petrus is an alchemist
who cannot see the future,
who, with Conquistadorial zeal
and as doomed as the Incas,
has dedicated his life to gold,

and all his wife can do is pray
to the Lord above
that one day
he'll convert
his dreams of wealth
to thoughts of love.

# The Wife's Peace Plan

This peace plan has been devised
to bring to an end ten years
of verbal violence, hurt and tears.

The main points –
from which there will be no deviation –
are as follows:

There will be separate beds in separate rooms.

In yours, so long as they're out of my sight,
you can look at your dirty mags and videos
as often as you like.

You will knock on my door and wait for an answer.

You will not enter my room
when I'm not there (except in emergencies).

I too, in the same way,
will respect both your territory and privacy.

The rest of the house will remain a free zone.
As before I'll keep it clean.
We will cook our own meals
at separate times in the kitchen.

The civilians (one son, two daughters)
will be allowed to live their lives free
from the constant threat of conflict.

We will put on an act if necessary.
They are scarred enough from this war as it is.

Dignitaries will still be received in the living room.
As agreed, we will sit with them as a couple –
laugh and chat
and lie through our teeth.

These are the ways in which we *will* keep the peace.

# Tom's Presentation

Clutching the company's newest product like a gun,
but going into battle green,
I quickly marched up on to the stage,
my head down, came to attention,
and then I talked,
talked in bursts of rapid gunfire,
my face lit up by panic
as if my mouth had just been set alight.

Unable to see the whites of eyes,
just the haze of fear in front of me,
I tried but could not pierce
the armoured plating of the interviewer's steely gaze.
I was shell-shocked, dazed,
stumbling over barbed words,
stuttering in the line of fire,
my face so red I felt as if it would explode;
I got through, came out alive, but only just –
or at least that's what I thought:

Dear *Tom*,

It is with deep regret we must inform you
of your recent death upon the battlefield,
at the rank of ex-potential Retail Assistant,
Grade: Presentation Stage (No Further);
This position is hereby confirmed on headed paper.

Yours sincerely,

*The manager*

The hundredth company to which you've applied.

Thomas McColl  **53**

# The Paper Round

I've left the estate 'til last today. Only three days doing this paper round, and I've already had enough.

I'm exhausted carrying the papers in the bag that, rolled up, become sticks of dynamite poking out of each letterbox.

The fuse is lit inside my head.

As always, the Connor boys are waiting there at the first turning and, trying to ignore their taunts, I say nothing back and draw the first rolled-up paper out of the bag just like a gun.

It's a lethal weapon in my darkest thoughts.

I have no bullets and they know it.

They come up and push me, tug at my coat, call me a girl, call me a poof, and one even kicks me hard in the leg.

I hate the job, hate the gang, and the adults who always remain behind closed doors.

As I do my round, each rolled up paper is a knife, each door the owner's chest, and getting rid of the stress, I thrust one through each letterbox.

# The Teacher's First Day

*"Tim, what have I just said?"*

The teacher casts the line across the room, and the tug of its hook wakes a minnow from its deep sea dream. The others turn to see the teacher's catch, that sits wide-eyed and gasping for answers.

*"I thought as much,"* says the teacher. *"John, what have I just said?"*

The great white shark stirs.

*"Fuck all, sir."*

It can smell the blood colouring the teacher's cheeks.

*"What did you say?"*

It waits calmly in its seat.

*"I said, what did you say?"*

Its teeth then cuts through the air that's thick with fear.

*"I said, fuck all, sir."*

The teacher, splashing about, at first speechlessly, finally blurts out: *"That's it, I'm getting the Head."*

He opens the classroom door and comes to the surface, feeling as if he's lost his legs. And, having already lost his face, knows full well that slamming the door behind him to shut out the rising currents of murmurs and giggles won't save him from drowning.

He's done for, and still able to feel the piercing stare of the shark's cold and lonely eyes, and the whole of his body being eaten alive, the teacher, unable now to even walk, collapses into a heap in the middle of the corridor.

# The World at One

The World at One –
The headlines on the hour:

The Earth's still going around the Sun.
No change: Still turning on its axis once every 24 hours.

Experts predict the situation
will remain this way for quite some time.

The PM's appealed for calm:
*"Go to work. Go about your normal business.*
*But use your time efficiently,*
*for time is passing constantly."*

The future's looking bleak.
Experts predict
365 days per year
until further notice.

*"Even accounting for the extra day*
*in each leap year,"*
says Vicky Hammond at the Harberg Institute,
*"with an average of only 70 years to live,*
*we'll all eventually die."*

Scientists cannot stop the aging process.

The President's been notified of this.

According to White House sources,
he will still go ahead
with his birthday as planned next week.

# Pervert

I've only been living here for five weeks
and already I've got a pervert climbing into my garden at
night
and hanging women's underwear on my washing line.

I've no idea who's doing this,
but all the villagers think the underwear is mine,
and seem to see it as some kind of sign,
a convenient excuse
to make me
the subject of intimidation and abuse.

Once again,
the postman has delivered his phlegm
through the letter box.

I've been left a black body bag
by the waste disposal men.

The council has granted my neighbours
the exceptional right
to play their music loud at night.

In the street, as they pass,
men make threats underneath their breath,
and children flee,
while women look at me with contempt and disgust.

Kids shout *"Pervert! Pervert!"*
as they push used condoms through my letter box.

The word PERVERT, in red paint,
has been daubed across my front door.

At night, I can see the silhouette of the hooded pervert,
accompanied now by a large gang,
all of them helping to place women's underwear on my
washing line,

and now it's me
who's beginning to see
it as some kind of sign.

Thomas McColl **57**

# The Revolution Will Not be Displayed

To create my now notorious painting that could change its image to reflect the viewer's personal taste, I arranged for the world-famous mind-reader, Frederick Finker (with painted palms) and my pet chameleon (with painted paws) to each make their mark, while a witch cast a spell to ensure the necessary fusion between cognisance, chameleon and canvas.

That it worked was nothing short of revolutionary, and I thought it would earn me a fortune – but all it's done is land me in jail.

At first, many people saw great beauty in the painting. These were the people who weren't offended by all the weird and wonderful crazy things which keep on popping up in all our minds.

But other people who came across the painting complained about the "disgusting" images they were seeing. I explained that it was themselves they were seeing, but that simply made them even angrier than they already were.

Then police raided the gallery and they saw disgusting images too.

At my trial, the prosecutor bellowed: *"How ridiculous and arrogant of this so-called artist to state it's our own blackened souls which are being portrayed on the canvas? It is the artist's degenerate mind and no-one else's!"*

In any event, found guilty of poisoning people's minds, I was sentenced to six months, suspended for two years. Then, after a national outcry – i.e. an orchestrated tabloid media campaign – my 'far too lenient' sentence was increased to a year, and no longer suspended…

...and nor was my painting, which the gallery had to straight-away take down and give away to be destroyed – which was shocking enough, but I hadn't expected the bastards would take my pet chameleon too. They did, however, and after a vet concluded the multi-coloured animal had been poisoned by the paint, it was destroyed just like the painting.

# Fruit 'n' veg

The vice squad manned a fruit 'n' veg stall on Berwick Street to trap a fruit fetish ring believed to have been involved in groping grapes, and the elaborate sting ensnared three members doing the strawberry squeeze, the bent banana stroke, and the apple shine.

*"Arrests only tip of iceberg lettuce"* screamed a tabloid headline. The papers warned this new breed of pervert was determined and astute, and had no trouble finding traders running stalls of ill-repute.

In Soho, one could tell prostitutes had found another service they could sell, when plastic luminous tomatoes replaced red light bulbs in windows.

And it was soon clear that fruit 'n' veg abuse was rife among the clergy too. It got so bad that the Church felt compelled to cancel celebration of the harvest festival, and the Archbishop of Canterbury was moved to make an impassioned plea: *"The Lord has given us fruit 'n' veg, not to play with, but to eat."*

The vice squad even had to arrest two bobbies on the beat: They were found sat in the lounge of a pub which had a back room where an illegal fruit 'n' veg show had only moments before been in full swing, and though claiming they'd entered the premises simply to hand out anti-knife crime leaflets, the officers had trouble explaining why each had a cucumber attached to his belt in place of his truncheon.

And it wasn't just police, but judges, lawyers and prominent politicians getting caught. It seemed like the very fabric of society was falling apart, and the PM's response was quick. He brought in severe penalties for fruit 'n' vegploitation.

In a speech, he made it clear: *"If you abuse the carrot you get the stick!"*

# Sunday Market

A corporate-burger-chomping part-time leftie, who's telling a trader he shouldn't sell Nestlé, fails to notice a pickpocket thief, his hands scarred by wallet rash, lifting all his cards and cash while the traders wink.

There's nothing much the blundering-as-a-blind-cyclops community cops can do. God-drilled tag-line preachers, at the market gates, shout: *"Money is not your God!"*, but the poor sod is cursed like a loan-shark collared giro mark, and leaves before he starts to cry, unable to bear being stared at by the harsh flea-market's compound eye.

The traders are far too busy pattering slackened minds with tat for kids and food that's out of date to have any time for some fast-food-chomsky telling them that the Nestlé Corp's immorally pushing sapped-breast substitution milk on Mozambican mothers.

*"It's all fallen off the back of a lorry, at any rate,"* says the Nestlé trader to his immediate neighbour, a woman who's baiting bric-a-brac to a grey-pound zombie crowd of OAPs with luddite tendencies, pursed bloodless lips and flat-earth stares. Even if some have overheard what's said, there's no-one here who cares. And locals know that the wallet-rash man never takes from them, only from outsiders.

# Security Camera

A security camera,

possessed
by ghost
of builder

who fell past lens
to sudden death
on Tuesday last,

has already started
loudly zooming
at the sight
of women
walking past.

# Jackpot

I am, along with hundreds of others,
the prize on this occasion.
And Oxford Circus
has the winning combination.

I'm reminded of a fruit machine
when the tube train
enters each station
and the posters on the wall
fly past the carriage window I'm facing.

When it slows to a stop,
through each window
I can see a poster
for a product or a shop,
which with the Oxford Circus sign,
on Saturday,
will win the jackpot every time.

Through my personal stereo headphones,
the Capital Radio DJ announces:

*"While traffic lights are down,*
*expect delays and congestion*
*round Oxford Circus station,*
*as the midday shoppers*
*flow like coins*
*from every exit*
*on to Oxford Street."*

# The Count

Despite the huge risk, the Count can't resist stepping out as a Countess, roaming the streets at night in a long black dress, caked in white foundation and blood-red lipstick.

It's rumoured that if any man is kissed on the neck by a cross-dressing vampire, the victim will be sucked dry of all his masculinity and, as a result, condemned for all eternity to having the insatiable urge to dress in women's clothes.

There's no truth in this scurrilous rumour. The Count isn't even a vampire – and nor were the three young transvestites burned at the stake last week. But, being as he now refuses to wear anything other than clothes befitting a Countess, the Count is forced to hide inside his fortified castle throughout the day – not because of the sun, but because of what he knows will be done to him by the angry transphobic towns-folk if he dares to step outside.

# The Beast in the Bag

She held it by the scruff of its neck,
and kept it at arm's length
as she walked around the side of the house to the bin.

Her son,
holed up in his room,
was now as shy
as what she'd found that morning
hidden away in his chest of drawers.

Disgusted by its slippery glossy skin,
she left it in the bag
as she tossed it in the bin,
unable to bear
to even glimpse again
this creature's feral femininity,
or think of her son's excited face
gawping at the sight of it,
or – in her rage – now think of it
as anything other than it,
a captured but still dangerous beast
that had only been prevented
from consuming her son
by the smooth protective glass of each page,
but had probably still managed somehow
to inject him with poison.

With a venomous look on her face,
she roughly shoved the bag
in between the larger bags of rubbish
piled up high in the bin,
burying the beast with a punch,
as if to kill it,
make sure it was dead,

but knowing deep down
she was no more going to win
this battle of wills
than the woman the creature had been created from,
an actual person, a human being
(who yet, somehow, was not)
who, after being exaggerated,
and made to appear to be a dangerous, uncontrollable beast,
had been – with just a single camera shot – extinguished.

# His Bad Side

His good side was allowed to politely refuse
the offers of old haggard prostitutes
still turning tricks
by the market stalls on Berwick Street,

but only because his bad side
demanded it be satisfied
by the woman whose card in the phone box read:
*"Suki. Sexy. 19, young and sweet."*

It was his bad side's ambition
that worked the long hours every week,
earning the right to decide
on how his cash would now be spent.

Suki turned out to be heaven-sent,
a fallen angel
who'd descended only as far
as the third floor of a posh flat
in a newly-built apartment block.

His good side did its job
and praised her beauty,
discussed the fee,
provided the pleasantries and small talk,
then when she began to undress in front of him,
his bad side muscled in,
finally able to let itself be free.

Within half an hour,
Suki had earned her fee.
His bad side was satisfied,
and back on the street,
was content now
to allow its better half to once again envelop it,
to hide it from the passers-by,
the passengers on the train,
the wife and kids.

# Wish You Were Here

My son's gone to Bethlehem. I hardly ever see him now these time machines are cheap and mass produced. All the kids want on the 25<sup>th</sup> is to see the first Christmas. That's why the inns are full, and a major construction firm is already there bulldozing shacks and replacing them with souvenir shops and hotels.

The BC natives stay well clear. They're convinced the cranes are dragons, and ever since a Roman regiment was routed by five builders in pickup trucks, the townsfolk live in fear and, each day, offer the metal monsters a virgin tied to a tree.

Without fail, the following day – albeit two thousand years later – a photo appears, on The Sun's page three, of a young Galilean woman, topless:

*"...BETHLEHEM BELTER – It's booby BC babe Betheba..."*

However, it isn't just sleazy tabloid paps and reporters taking advantage of the complete deregulation of time, but reporters from all the more serious papers too – who've sometimes returned with some shocking exclusives: It's been revealed, for instance, that Stalin was originally a third rate hack from the Morning Star – and born in Gorleston, not Gori, Georgia – and that Hitler wasn't born in Braunau but in Braintree, and started out as a Daily Express cartoonist.

And while everyone's reeling still from finding out that all the terrible events of the past were actually shaped by people from the future, it's just been revealed that the Cerne Giant, the Uffington White Horse, and even the cave paintings at Lascaux, were all in fact created by anonymous wannabe Banksys...

...and all of them are under the age of 20. In fact, according to figures just out, over 80 per cent of so-called history hackers are teens.

*"...A new type of hackavist – having conquered the almost infinite internet – is now hacking into the infinite past..."* reports a BBC news correspondent – live from the past.

Still, it's ironic that children and young people – who have, by far, the most time on their hands – are the ones most desperate now to stretch every spare second they have by travelling back and forth through time.

Though still shy of his seventeenth birthday, my son's already dating one of the dancers at Chicago's Tropic Club in 1932 and, at the same but different time, is dating Cleopatra too. It bothers me, but I tolerate his trips so long as they're in well-known makes of time machine. What else can I do? Parents can't control their kids. I've even heard that self-assembly kits, imported from China, are now being sold outside school gates. The last thing I want is my son to use inferior makes.

It's now believed that thousands of missing children have fallen victim to faulty machines that, hurtling into the past, will never again return.

# The Full Stop Rebellion

Full stops will go on strike from
9pm this Monday night
in protest at being constantly forced
to prop up dictatorial statements
and provide their round signatures
to half-truths and outright lies.

This strike will affect both speech and print.
Commas can't be relied upon.
Some may strike in support.

The public should refrain from non-essential
speaking, writing, typing and reading.
There is the real possibility of death
from not being able to pause for breath.

The chattering classes have been warned
that the choice could be as stark as shut up or die.

Hospitals are on standby.
Emergency wards have this week
been stocked with large consignments
of compliant full stops,
imported from Qatar,
for use in life saving sentences
(It's believed that Britain's
'good friend' in the Gulf
will get a dozen new tanks
by way of thanks
for stepping in so quickly with supplies).

*

News just in –
The Government is rushing through a new law
to elevate the status of the colon.

*"It makes perfect sense,"* insists the Prime Minister.
*"Two dots are clearly more of a full stop than one dot."*

No-one knows yet though if demotion of the full stop
will avert the looming crisis:

# The End: Lesson Learnt

:

# Acknowledgements

Acknowledgements are due to the editors of the following, in which some of these poems have appeared:

Magazines: *the Affectionate Punch, Aireings, the Alarmist, Ape, Belleville Park Pages, the Big Spoon, Breathe, the Coffee House, Community of Poets, Envoi, Equinox, Fire, Global Tapestry Journal, Hand Job Zine, Here Comes Everyone, the Incubator Journal, Ink, Sweat and Tears, Iota, Lateral Moves, the Literary Commune, London Literary Project, Marco Polo Arts Mag, the Molotov Cocktail, Monkey Kettle, Nasty Piece of Work, Neon Highway, Never Bury Poetry, Oblong, Open Pen, Paper & Ink Zine, Paragraph Planet, Patchword, Piffle, the Platform, Poetry Monthly, Poetry Nottingham International, Purple Patch, Push, Rain Dog, Ramraid Extraordinaire, the Ranfurly Review, Renegade, Rising, the Rue Bella, Running Water, Shift, Sierra Heaven, Slipstream, Stand Up Tragedy, Unthunk Journal, Volume.*

Anthologies:

The World at One – *Our World (Co-op Caring Poetry Festival 1995)*
In Search of Pedestrianland – *Direct Axiom (Reclaim the Streets 1996)*
Muslim Girl at the Bus Stop – *In the Company of Poets (Hearing Eye 2003)*
Takeaway Poetry Joint – *Scraps (National Flash Fiction Day anthology 2013)*

'The Nose Picker: Public Enemy Number One' won 2nd prize in *4'33" magazine's* 60 Second Story Contest (May 2012)

'Jackpot' was featured in poster form in the *Poetry on Walls* 'Movement' exhibition at the Union Chapel, Islington (8th to 23rd March 1996)